LOCAL DEVELOPMENT STRATEGIES

Diosey Ramon Lugo-Morin

Preface

The importance of local development strategies lies in several aspects: ***economic development***: These strategies enable the utilization of local resources, stimulate job creation, strengthen the local business fabric, and encourage investment in the community. By promoting local economic development, socio-economic inequalities are reduced, and opportunities for progress and prosperity are generated. ***Citizen participation***: Local development strategies involve local stakeholders, such as residents, community organizations, businesses, and local authorities, in decision-making and project implementation. This strengthens citizen participation, promotes community empowerment, and ensures that actions are relevant and aligned with local needs and aspirations. ***Environmental sustainability***: The local focus allows for consideration of the region's natural environment characteristics and peculiarities. Local development strategies aim to promote sustainable practices, such as efficient resource use, environmental protection, and the adoption of renewable energy sources. This contributes to environmental conservation, the reduction of negative impacts, and improved resilience to environmental challenges. ***Cultural and social identity:*** Local development strategies value and preserve the cultural and social identity of the community. They foster the development of cultural activities, the strengthening of local traditions, and the promotion of cultural heritage. This generates a sense of belonging and pride among inhabitants, contributing to social cohesion and emotional well-being. ***Economic diversification:*** Local development strategies aim to diversify the local economy to reduce dependency on a single sector or industry. This helps decrease vulnerability to economic crises and creates a more dynamic and resilient business environment. Additionally, economic diversification can foster innovation and the development of emerging sectors.

Local development strategies are crucial for driving inclusive economic growth, strengthening social cohesion, preserving the environment, and promoting community well-being. By focusing on the specific characteristics and needs of each region, these strategies can generate more effective and sustainable long-term outcomes. Certainly, let's analyze the case of Venezuela to illustrate the importance of local development strategies. Venezuela is a country that has faced significant economic, social, and political challenges in recent years. The implementation of effective local development strategies could play a crucial role in addressing these issues and promoting sustainable growth.

Economic development: Venezuela has traditionally relied heavily on oil exports, which has made its economy vulnerable to fluctuations in oil prices. Local development strategies could focus on diversifying the economy by promoting the development of other sectors, such as agriculture, tourism, and manufacturing, in different regions of the country. This would reduce the country's dependence on oil and create new job opportunities, contributing to economic stability and prosperity at the local level.

Citizen participation: In Venezuela, citizen participation in decision-making processes has been limited, leading to a lack of ownership and accountability. Local development strategies that actively involve local communities, organizations, and businesses in the planning and implementation of projects would empower citizens and ensure that initiatives meet their specific needs. This participatory approach would foster a sense of belonging and collective responsibility, ultimately strengthening social cohesion.

Environmental sustainability: Venezuela is known for its rich biodiversity and natural resources. However, unsustainable practices, such as deforestation and unregulated mining, have resulted in environmental degradation. Local development strategies could prioritize the preservation of natural habitats, the promotion of sustainable agricultural practices, and the adoption of clean energy technologies. By integrating environmental considerations into local development plans, Venezuela can protect its ecosystems and create a more sustainable future.

Cultural and social identity: Venezuela is a culturally diverse country with a rich heritage. Local development strategies could prioritize the preservation and promotion of cultural traditions, art, and tourism. This would not only enhance the cultural identity of different regions but also create opportunities for cultural tourism, which can contribute to economic growth and job creation while fostering a sense of pride and appreciation for the country's diverse cultural heritage.

Economic diversification: Venezuela's heavy reliance on oil exports has left it vulnerable to economic shocks. Local development strategies that support the development of alternative sectors, such as agribusiness, renewable energy, and technology, would diversify the economy and reduce its susceptibility to external factors. This diversification would stimulate innovation, entrepreneurship, and economic resilience, leading to a more sustainable and prosperous future.

The case of Venezuela highlights the significance of local development strategies in addressing economic, social, and environmental challenges. By prioritizing economic diversification, citizen participation, environmental sustainability, and the preservation of cultural identity, local development strategies can contribute to the country's overall development and improve the well-being of its citizens. Starting from the importance of formulating local development strategies, this book aims to be an initial guide to promote the territories of Venezuela, it presents a methodology that addresses various aspects of development. From this perspective, Venezuela can empower its rural areas, improve the quality of life of rural communities, increase economic opportunities and create sustainable and inclusive development in the country.

Table of Contents

Chapter I

INTRODUCTION

Venezuela is currently undergoing profound social changes, especially in rural areas. These changes are aimed at promoting agricultural and rural development with a legal structure adequate to the current challenges, with financial resources and, most importantly, with highly trained human resources. The changes have three main aspects: reducing poverty levels, generating sustainable employment, and guaranteeing food sovereignty, all based on social justice.

Due to the crisis in the countryside, at the end of the 1990s, a new government took the reins of power led by Hugo Chávez Frías, and reforms began with the drafting and approval of a new constitution, and new structures were created to design and promote rural development, among which the following stand out: The National Land Institute, the National Institute for Rural Development, and the Agricultural Bank. Highlighting the role of these institutions in the Venezuelan rural space, some strategic elements are highlighted within a local analytical framework.

The establishment of the National Land Institute initiated a policy of democratisation of land ownership. Since 2000, more than 70,000 cooperatives have been organised; nearly 50% of them are aimed at strengthening and promoting the agro-productive sector. In addition, more than 3,600,000 hectares of land have been handed over to small and medium-sized farmers with landholding patterns ranging from 5 ha to 50 ha. An aggressive financing plan was implemented for small and medium farmers, whereby land was provided with credit. In 2004, the government allocated one billion dollars to the agro-productive sector, with an emphasis on small and medium farmers. For 2006, financing for the agro-productive sector is 40 billion bolivars (calculated with 2006 dollars).

The Land and Agrarian Development Law was enacted in 2001. This law seeks a fair distribution of wealth and a strategic, democratic, and participatory planning of land tenure and the development of all agricultural activities. In 2005, the government enacted the decree for the reorganisation of land tenure and use of agricultural land (INTi, 2006), whereby large tracts of land that are idle (if the land belongs to the state) or unproductive (if the land is private) will be redistributed to the entire landless peasant population.

These changes in Venezuelan agrarian reform have brought with them, since 2000, a significant distribution of the nation's land to peasants and indigenous people, and along with the land, financial support to work it.

In this sense, the Venezuelan agrarian structure, following the implementation of the Land and Agricultural Development Law, has undergone important changes. These began with a massive regularisation of land and, to a lesser extent, the endowment of land. From 2004 to the present, the phenomenon has changed, with a significant increase in land endowment and a decrease in regularisation. This situation is relevant because peasants and indigenous Venezuelans are now in the countryside and are in possession of the nation's land. In addition, the number of new peasants has increased significantly with the implementation of the decree for the reorganisation of land tenure and use of agricultural land. Moreover, they have access to financing to work their land. However, although this horizon seems ideal, regressive social phenomena occur within it, phenomena that are not basically focused on the structuralism of the state, but are centred on the peasant and the indigenous, focusing on a set of unsatisfied needs that do not guarantee their reproduction strategies, which they try to solve through development projects and programmes generated by the technician, without the participation of the peasant in the majority of cases, an observation that coincides with the study by Freire (1998).

Robledo Hernández (2002), point out that the concept of reproductive strategies refers to the set of conscious or unconscious actions or practices that peasant families deploy to guarantee their survival. On the other hand, Méndez Espinosa, (2005) emphasises that the interdependence of the productive and consumer functions of the peasant household group is embodied in the analytical category of "reproduction strategy", which articulates the objectives of the group with the alternative ways it can develop towards that end. To understand the strategies followed by peasant families, it is necessary to consider the characteristics of the local space in which they are inserted, since this is the framework in which the interaction of the groups and their differentiated access to means of production takes place. Bautista (2004), when referring to reproduction strategies, establishes a relationship between the set of tasks or activities carried out by the domestic unit and the ways to counteract its disadvantageous position in the market and allow it to survive.

Díaz Tepepa et al. (2004) point out that the Western technical world has forgotten that peasant and indigenous producers and their families are social actors capable of generating and transmitting knowledge, of accumulating experience, of inventing, innovating, and experimenting, in short of creating culture in their eternal task of extracting goods from nature. Díaz Tepepa et al. (2004) stresses that this is due to a false belief that rural cultures are inferior to technicians and researchers from urban-industrial centres, and also to the idea that conventional or contemporary science is the only valid knowledge for solving the problems of nature management (the fundamental thesis of scientism, i.e. science turned into ideology).

This scientism is leading to a kind of blindness to understand that in the management of natural resources there is not only the application of science and modern techniques, but also a wealth of practical and concrete experiences represented by the personal or community wisdoms of traditional producers with which the human species has managed to reproduce its material conditions throughout history (Díaz Tepepa et al., 2004).

The National Institute for Rural Development (INDER) was created by mandate of the Law of Land and Agrarian Development on November 9, 2001, with the objective of contributing to the integral rural development of the agricultural sector in: Infrastructure, Training and Extension. It is an autonomous institute, attached to the Ministry of Agriculture and Lands, with legal personality and its own assets, distinct and independent from the Republic. Its current national headquarters are in the city of Guanare, Portuguesa state, and it operates in a decentralised manner in 23 regional and state offices, each one faithfully fulfilling its responsibilities to carry out its main objectives (INDER, 2006).

The competencies of the institution include: 1) to direct, coordinate and execute the national policies and plans linked to irrigation and land reclamation, established by the National Executive; 2) to promote and ensure the sustainable use of water resources in irrigation systems; 3) to promote, direct, execute and maintain the infrastructure of rural support services owned by the State, for the production and transformation of agri-food items; 3) Promote, direct, execute and maintain the infrastructure of rural support services owned by the State, for the production and transformation of agri-foodstuffs; 4) Promote the construction of infrastructure works aimed at extending irrigated land, for which purpose it shall promote the establishment of a coordinating commission with the competent bodies in the matter; 5) To promote, coordinate and implement plans and programmes aimed at establishing forms of regional, municipal and local organisation for the common use of water; 6) To promote, coordinate and implement plans and programmes aimed at the organisation and consolidation of rural communities, through the various associative forms of self-management, management and co-management contemplated in the laws; 8) Promote the creation of organisations for the self-management, management and co-management of irrigation systems and land reclamation (INDER, 2006).

The National Institute for Rural Development, when incorporated into the Ministry of Agriculture and Lands, has taken on the challenge of planning with justice and social equity to include rural men and women in the country's productive process. Understanding that rural development cannot be seen only as the construction of hydro-agricultural infrastructure works, we assumed with responsibility the ten objectives set out in the "New Strategic Map" and we deepened the work of training and organisation with rural producers through the Indigenous Peoples and Community Development Management Offices (INDER, 2006).

Finally, the creation of the Agricultural Bank of Venezuela, an institution that initially had a capital of 40 billion bolivars that will be increased by contributions from the Executive, which will be granted to approximately 3 million small and medium producers and agricultural workers and thus cover their financing needs (INTi, 2006).

On 19 November 2014, Decree No. 1,400 a legal instrument designed to promote the socio-productive model with a predominance of social property as the framework for the new production relations in the agricultural sector.

The Venezuelan rural space possesses the elements (labour force, local knowledge, dynamic markets, institutional support, and financing) to face the global changes that Latin America is currently facing; it is only necessary to strengthen the immense human capital that the Venezuelan countryside currently occupies. For this reason, I believe it is necessary to build methodological tools that promote and encourage local development from a perspective centred on the social subject.

The objective of the present work is to provide a theoretical and methodological analysis tool that allows the technician to identify the potential of the social subjects (peasant and indigenous) and their respective domestic units of the Venezuelan rural space and in function of this, to be able to elaborate local development strategies.

Chapter II

THEORETICAL-CONCEPTUAL FRAMEWORK

In Latin America there have been important efforts to develop methodological analysis tools for the elaboration of local development strategies, the first one was developed by Dr. Leobardo Jiménez Sánchez of the College of Postgraduate Studies, Mexico and authority on the subject, he devised and executed the Plan Puebla, whose philosophy was based on the premise that man is the motive and end of all creative activity. In man reside the values, the vitality, and the intellectual and physical capacity to solve the problems imposed by the physical, economic and social environment. Another correlative premise is that the solution to many of these problems requires an organised effort by the members of society and that the capacity to solve them can also be developed in the less advantaged sectors (Martínez Valdez, 1970).

Other more recent experiences are those of the Latin American and Caribbean Institute for Economic and Social Planning (ILPES) (Silva Lira, 2003; ILPES, 1998), the Chilean government through the Subsecretaría de Desarrollo Regional y Administrativa also has an important experience, but more oriented towards territorial management (MIC, 2004). The contributions and experiences are valuable tools for the elaboration of development strategies at local and regional level; however, I would like to point out that the approach used is basically structuralist, leaving aside the importance of peasants and indigenous people as the main generators of empirical strategies. Another relevant experience is that implemented by the European Union through its LEADER development programme (EU, 2000a, 2000b, 2001; Canzanelli, 2004), which has focused its efforts on a revalorisation of the European rural space.

The Venezuelan rural space: some elements for its understanding

Before the arrival of the Hispanic population, the current Venezuelan territory was the seat of multiple and varied ethnic contingents that had to adapt to different geographical and ecological environments. In this process, the nature-culture dialectic adopted different ways of expression that allowed man to adapt to the conditions of the environment, creating techniques and instruments that responded to the needs and expectations of these indigenous groups. The socio-economic dynamics of these communities were related to the development of neighbouring cultural areas, thus generating an interaction that contributed to diversifying and enriching their means of subsistence and their overall cultural heritage (Ríos and Carvallo, 1990).

Historical, ethno-historical and archaeological studies have identified six areas that constitute the main focal points for the concentration of populations with cultural affinities between them. These are: the area of the Orinoco and its tributaries, the area of the central-eastern Caribbean coast, the area of the Andean mountain range, the area of the western Andean foothills, the north-western area, and the Guajira area. The Hispanic relationship with the ethnic groups would end up halting and altering the historical course of the latter, by disorganising and demographically diminishing them, and by subsuming them with other demographic and socio-cultural factors in a syncretism that resulted in the Venezuelan social conformation (Ríos and Carvallo, 1990).

In the six cultural geographic areas that make it possible to appreciate the varied societal spectrum of pre-Hispanic Venezuela, it is possible to distinguish two fundamental models of socio-economic organisation. One of these corresponds to the productive forms and socio-political organisational matrices adopted by most of the groups established in the lowland areas of the territory. These populations were characterised by an undeveloped techno-economy in which itinerant agriculture coexisted with hunting, fishing, and the gathering of vegetables and/or marine molluscs. This mode of production, which did not generate an economic surplus of political or social significance, ranged from nomadic groups with a simple family structure to semi-permanent sedentary conglomerates with more formal political and social ties. The second modality refers to the populations of the Andean area and certain groups in the northwestern region. These aboriginal communities put into practice a type of rationality in land use and in the organisation of agricultural productive activity, as well as a set of techniques that allowed them to master water resources to improve agricultural production and guarantee a relatively high volume of surpluses (Ríos and Carvallo, 1990). The indigenous human groups that occupied Venezuelan territory for thousands of years through successive migrations had to try out different technological responses to the subsistence problems posed by a very varied environment. In this way, from cultural forms strongly conditioned by environmental factors, it was possible to arrive at situations in which man possessed a certain capacity to control and modify the dynamics of the ecological environment according to his survival needs. The first signs of agricultural activity date back to the second millennium

B.C., in the northwestern sector of Lake Maracaibo, because of the cultural contributions of certain populations settled in Central and South America. But the generalisation of the new sedentary way of life based on agriculture began between the 11th and 7th centuries BC, in the vicinity of the lower Orinoco, relegating hunting, fishing, and gathering activities to less significance in the subsistence base (Ríos and Carvallo, 1990).

The development of agriculture in Venezuelan territory was a staggered and asynchronous process that was simultaneously conditioned by the physical and ecological characteristics of each region and the socio-cultural traits of each ethnic group. The selection and sowing of certain types of crops resulted in certain varieties becoming dominant in certain regions for reasons of yield and adaptation to agro-ecological conditions. This in turn had an impact on the social structuring of human groups. Although agricultural sedentarisation reached practically the whole of the pre-Columbian human conglomerates that occupied the Venezuelan space, it is possible to delimit certain zones that, due to the peculiarity of their ecosystems, gathered a set of basic elements for subsistence and, therefore, favoured the establishment of this new form of production and collective and individual relationship with the environment. In this sense, we can point to the valleys of the coastal mountain range, the flat north-western areas, and the Andean mountain range (Ríos and Carvallo, 1990).

The diversification introduced by agriculture into the individual-community-habitat relationship broadened the cultural panorama of the indigenous groups, serving as a basis for the establishment of new patterns of human ecology, which shifted from excessive environmental specialisation to a greater capacity to adapt to different ecosystems. The agricultural practices of the indigenous Venezuelans located in these areas were characterised by their tendency to conserve the environmental balance. Following this orientation, procedures based on natural fertilisation of soils and natural weed control were put into practice. The predominant form of agriculture was swidden, characterised by polyculture and intensive farming. Therefore, the technological transformations that occurred in the Venezuelan area before the arrival of the Spanish were not sufficiently profound to generate a radical change in the structure and cultural level of the aboriginal societies, as happened in some civilisations in South and Mesoamerica, but in terms of the use or organisation of space, the human groups located in the Venezuelan area managed to develop an empirical knowledge of the environment and its dynamics, as well as a technological heritage, which although they reached modest proportions, had great significance as criteria of cultural ecology, to the extent that they guaranteed the ecological balance and the recovery of renewable natural resources (Ríos and Carvallo, 1990).

A study by Molina (1996), taking as a spatial unit of reference the political-territorial division at the level of federal entities, shows the spatial patterns in terms of dominant location and their temporal trends. He points out that the spatial patterns of Venezuelan agriculture are characterised by multiple patterns, with variable temporal trends.

In the agricultural sector, mechanised annual crops, which include the cereal, oilseed, and legume groups, presented concentrated patterns in terms of dominant location for most crops. Most of the states that participate in the harvested area are in the Venezuelan plains (central, western, and eastern). The federal entities that appear most frequently as dominant locations are Guárico and Portuguesa, for cereals, and Portuguesa, Anzoategui, and Barinas for oilseeds. In contrast to these two groups, leguminous crops show patterns that between 1970 and 1990 have varied from moderately dispersed to dual. The concentration in the first two groups (cereals and oilseeds) is related to the predominance of the mechanised annual crop production system, while beans and beans are reproduced in many entities under the subsistence and semi-commercial production system (Molina, 1996).

In the commercial horticulture system, there are slight differences in the changes in the dominant location between high-floor and low-floor vegetables. In the case of high-floor vegetables, the dominant location patterns are concentrated and moderately concentrated, with a decrease in the harvested area of garlic, carrots, and potatoes in the states of Tachira, Merida and Trujillo, with a certain geographical continuity, except for potatoes, where the presence of Lara, Carabobo and Aragua as important producers is due to the introduction of varieties adapted to higher temperatures in these states. The relative importance of these varieties has been such that Lara has displaced the traditional potato-producing states. Tomato and paprika went from being moderately concentrated in 1970 to dual in 1990, since there has been a rearrangement of the distribution of the harvested area, which shows the increase in the relative importance of Lara and Aragua States as producers. Nevertheless, an important percentage of the harvested area, close to 50%, is distributed in a dispersed manner. As for the dominant location, for paprika, in addition to Lara and Aragua, the State of Falcón should be mentioned; in the case of tomato, in recent years, its relative participation has increased in the

States of Portuguesa and Guárico. The classification inherent to the trend between 1970 and 1990 showed a predominance of dynamic patterns (garlic, carrot, tomato), moderately dynamic (potato and onion) and very dynamic (paprika). In all crops there were absolute increases in the harvested area, which can be explained mainly by the installation of irrigation systems in the high valleys of the Andean region by the Corporación de Los Andes and by private irrigation works in the case of low-floor vegetables (Molina, 1996).

The spatial patterns of the crops classified within the plantation system, such as coffee and cocoa, do not show variations in the dominant location. Coffee is located in the states of Táchira, Mérida, Trujillo and Sucre, and contributed between 52% (1970) and 54% (1990) of the total harvested area; the rest of the area is distributed in a dispersed manner (less than 10%) in 12 other states. Cocoa is found in Sucre and Miranda, which account for 87% of the total area. Bananas and plantains maintain their respective dominant location patterns over time. Bananas are dispersed, with 21 federal entities among the producers. Bananas show a dual pattern, with Zulia accounting for 48% (1970) and 52% (1990) of the harvested area. Sugar cane shows a moderately concentrated pattern that does not change over time. Four federal entities (Portuguesa, Yaracuy, Lara, and Aragua) account for 84% of the harvested area. The distribution of the area is highly related to the location of the sugar mills and the agro-ecological requirements of the crop. Pineapple changed its pattern between 1970 and 1990 from moderately concentrated to dual. Thus, while in 1970 there were four states among the most important producers (Lara, Trujillo, Carabobo, and Táchira), in 1990, only Lara accounted for 50% of the harvested area in the country (Molina, 1996).

In the animal sector, the cattle, pasture, and milk sectors are dominated by a dual pattern, except in the case of natural pasture, which is classified as moderately concentrated. The cattle population is 48% concentrated in three states (Zulia, Apure, and Guarico), while the remaining 52% is spread over 17 states. In terms of natural pastures, Apure, Bolivar, Guarico, and Barinas are the states with the largest areas, together accounting for 65% of the total surface area. The state of Zulia accounts for 53% of the total cultivated pastureland and contributes 66% of national milk production. With reference to pig farming, the herds are managed under intensive systems. The pattern varied from concentrated to moderately dispersed. In 1970, four entities (Miranda, Distrito Federal, Aragua and Carabobo) accounted for 90% of the herd, in 1990, two entities (Aragua and Miranda) accounted for 39% of the herd and the remaining percentage

(61%) was distributed in 17 entities. In the poultry category, the spatial pattern varied over time, remaining moderately concentrated between 1970 and 1990. Miranda, Aragua, Carabobo, and Zulia stand out as the entities with the dominant location (Molina, 1996).

The strategy concept and its formulation

The concept of strategy has its origins in military history and warfare. Throughout history, military commanders and strategists developed various approaches and plans to achieve victory in battles and wars. The term "strategy" itself derives from the Greek word "strategia," which means "generalship" or "the art of the general."

Ancient civilizations, such as the Greeks, Romans, and Chinese, recognized the importance of strategy in warfare. Prominent military leaders like Sun Tzu in ancient China and Thucydides in ancient Greece wrote influential treatises on strategy and warfare, which provided insights into the principles and tactics of successful military campaigns.

Over time, the concept of strategy extended beyond the realm of warfare and found applications in other domains, including politics, business, and sports. The principles and methodologies that were originally developed for military strategy became adapted and applied to these other areas. In the business context, strategy refers to a plan of action designed to achieve specific goals or objectives in a competitive environment. It involves making decisions regarding resource allocation, market positioning, product development, and other factors to gain a competitive advantage over rivals.

Today, the concept of strategy is studied and applied in various disciplines, becoming a fundamental concept for understanding and navigating complex systems and achieving long-term success in different fields, its importance in today's world is due to the following reasons:

Complex and Dynamic Environment: The modern world is characterized by complexity, uncertainty, and rapid change. Organizations and individuals face a wide range of challenges, such as globalization, technological advancements, economic shifts, and social and political disruptions. Developing and implementing effective strategies helps navigate this complex environment, make informed decisions, and adapt to changing circumstances.

Competitive Advantage: In a highly competitive landscape, having a well-defined strategy is crucial for gaining a competitive edge. Whether in business, politics, sports, or other fields, a strategy allows individuals and organizations to differentiate themselves, identify their unique strengths, exploit opportunities, and effectively respond to competitive pressures.

Goal Achievement: Strategies provide a roadmap for achieving specific goals or objectives. They help identify the steps, resources, and actions required to reach desired outcomes. By setting clear goals and developing a strategy to accomplish them, individuals and organizations can align their efforts and stay focused on what matters most.

Resource Optimization: Resources, whether financial, human, or material, are often limited and need to be utilized efficiently. Strategy helps optimize the allocation and utilization of resources by identifying priorities, making informed decisions about resource allocation, and minimizing waste or duplication of efforts.

Risk Management: Strategies assist in managing risks and uncertainties. By anticipating potential challenges and developing contingency plans, individuals and organizations can mitigate risks, minimize negative impacts, and seize opportunities that arise from unexpected events.

Long-Term Sustainability: Strategy provides a framework for long-term sustainability and growth. It encourages individuals and organizations to consider the broader impacts of their actions, adopt sustainable practices, and balance short-term gains with long-term viability and success.

Alignment and Focus: Strategy helps align individuals and organizations around a common purpose, vision, and direction. It provides clarity and focus, ensuring that efforts and resources are directed towards shared goals, reducing fragmentation and enhancing overall effectiveness.

Adaptability and Innovation: Effective strategies embrace adaptability and innovation. They encourage a proactive approach to change, foster a culture of learning and experimentation, and enable individuals and organizations to continuously evolve and stay relevant in a rapidly changing world.

The concept of strategy provides a structured approach to navigating complexity, gaining competitive advantage, achieving objectives, optimising resources, managing risks, ensuring long-term sustainability, and promoting adaptability and innovation. By applying strategic thinking and planning, individuals and organisations can increase their chances of success and thrive in today's dynamic and challenging environment.

According to Tse-Tung (1967), it is the study of the laws of military leadership that influence the war situation. The author points out that for the person in overall command, the most important thing is to concentrate his attention on the war situation as a whole; the commander, at whatever level, must primarily concentrate his attention on the most important and decisive problems or actions for the whole situation within the sphere of his activity, and not on other problems or actions. In determining what is important and decisive, one should not start from general or abstract circumstances, but from the concrete circumstances. In a military operation, the direction and point of assault must be chosen according to the situation of the enemy, the character of the terrain and the state of one's own forces at the given moment.

Tse-Tung (1967) points out that a strategy is formulated by taking from experience what can be applied today and working out something of one's own in the light of present conditions. Moreover, the author highlights five aspects to be considered when evaluating a strategy: the way, the time, the terrain, the command, and the discipline.

The way means ensuring that the purpose of the command and that of the troops is the same, so that in sharing life and death there is no fear of danger. When cheerful confidence is maintained in hardship, we forget death. If the troops are handled with benevolence and fairness, they will be loyal and will naturally identify themselves with the interests of the leaders.

Terrain must be assessed in terms of distance, difficulty or ease of movement, size, and security. The first thing to consider is the condition of the terrain. With the relevant data, it will be safe to manoeuvre, since the advantages and disadvantages that the troops will have in action are known. The necessary number of troops and the relative safety of the environment in which they will operate will be known.

As for command, intelligence, honesty, humanity, courage, and severity must be considered. Ancient kings considered humanity to be paramount. Strategists, on the other hand, have believed that intelligence comes first, for it is intelligence that enables them to make good plans and make changes on the fly. Mu Du explains that humanity consists of love and compassion for people, just as courage is recognised in the way one seizes opportunities to achieve victory without hesitation, and severity in the appropriate way of establishing discipline at all levels through strict punishments.

Honesty gives the troops confidence and, at the same time, security of time or punishment. Courage allows unloving action and severity establishes discipline. However, confidence in intelligence can result in rebellion; too much humanity in weakness; too much confidence can end in insanity; too much courage leads to violence and too severe orders to cruelty. The good leader is trained in the proper use of these virtues.

Discipline means organisation and the establishment of a chain of command and logistics.

For Mintzberg (1991), strategy is a process, which involves more than a simple set of recipes called "planning" with which it is generally associated, its objective is to respond to a changing situation, for those organisations that manage under past patterns without projecting into the future. For the author, a strategy is formulated considering a past of corporate capabilities and a future of market opportunities.

Mintzberg (1991) highlights two ways to understand the concept of strategy; in the first way, imagine someone planning strategy. What is most likely to spring to mind is the image of orderly thinking: a senior manager, or a group of them, sitting in an office formulating courses of action that everyone else will implement according to the timetable. The fundamental idea is reason, rational control, systematic analysis of competition and markets, of the strengths and weaknesses of the company or institution, and that the combination of these analyses produces clear, explicit, done, and right strategies. In the second aspect, now imagine someone who is handcrafting the strategy.

It is probably a completely different picture, as different from planning as craftsmanship is from mechanisation. Craftsmanship evokes traditional skill, dedication, perfection through mastery of detail. What comes to mind is not so much thought and reason as involvement, a feeling of intimacy and harmony with the materials at hand, developed through long experience and dedication. Formulation and execution merge in a fluid process of learning, through which creative strategies emerge. From the author's position, he stresses that the image of craftsmanship best captures the process through which effective strategies come to life. The planning image, popular for so long in the literature, distorts these processes and thus disorients organisations that embrace it wholeheartedly.

For the author, strategy starts from two elements; plans and patterns of the past and its nature lies in the intimate connection between thought and action, key aspects of strategy making (strategy is a word that is generally associated with the future, its link to the past is no less crucial). As Kierkegaard once observed, life is lived forwards but understood backwards). A strategy may emerge unexpectedly in response to a changing situation, or it may be deliberately provoked, through a process of formulation followed by its practice. But when these planned projects do not produce the desired actions, organisations are left with unrealised strategies. Effective strategies can surface in the strangest places and develop in the most unexpected ways. There is no better way to strategize; strategy is the mastery of detail.

For the purposes of this paper, strategy represents a set of coordinated actions aimed at solving a problem.

To elaborate a strategy, we need to have a starting point: the problem.

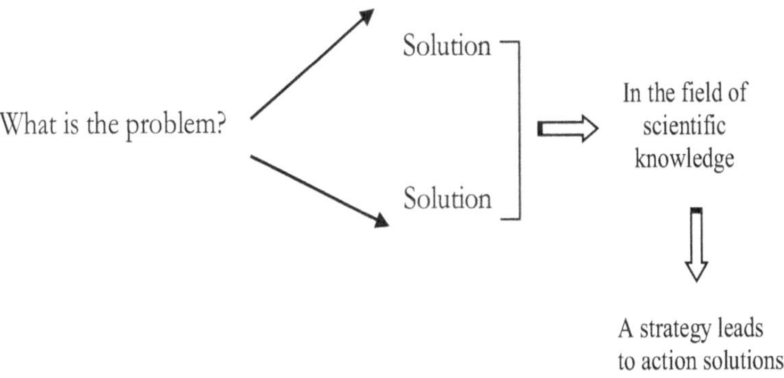

A problem is what is giving us the opportunity to find a possible solution. It is important not to confuse facts with problems. In the resolution of a problem there are social actors who want to find a solution and there are those who do not want a solution, the strategy is built with both actors.

In a problem there will be two relevant aspects: the means to solve it and the subject. The means (knowledge and strategy) are what will demand to be in one or the other field (referring to empiricism and scientism), ideally complementing each other. The subject is in a situation of looking for solutions to a problem.

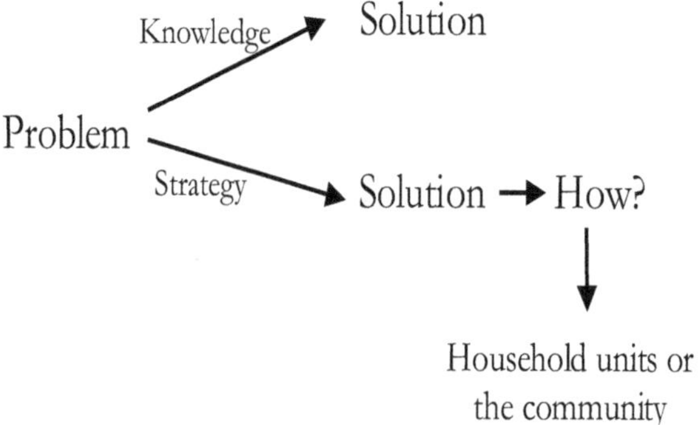

Key question when formulating a strategy

How: the members of the household unit or community have come up with the solution to the problem .... It is important to emphasise that each social subject understands the problems and their solutions in their own context. Man, lives immersed in problems, whether he creates them or not, he lives them and solves them.

Indigenous households are more stable in terms of knowledge, due to their constant presence in their territories. There are two types of strategies: Conflict: Where the means of finding a solution to the problem is that someone has to win, and someone has to lose. The capacity of each party and the means available to them to see the other is recognised. Coordination: In both parties there is a consensus to solve the problem, capacities and means of the collective are united to achieve the solution.

We assume that all the strategies to be formulated must be conflictual due to the differentiated structure of the social actors. In this sense, Bourdieu (2002) emphasises that social science does not have to construct classes, but rather social spaces within which classes can be differentiated, but which do not exist on paper. In each case, it must construct and discover the principle of differentiation that allows the empirically observed social space to be theoretically re-engendered.

All societies present themselves as social spaces, i.e., structures of differences that can only be truly understood if the generating principle that grounds these differences in objectivity is elaborated.

If all societies present themselves as social spaces defined by fields of power, there will be common elements (positions and dispositions of the social actors) in all of them, which will allow us to determine their nature. Therefore, it is possible to construct an explanatory model of the phenomena that occur within them based on the premises.

The field of power; it is the space of power relations between the different types of capital or, more precisely, between the subjects who are sufficiently endowed with one of the different types of capital to be in a position to dominate the corresponding field and whose struggles intensify whenever the relative value of the different types of capital (cultural capital, social capital, political capital and economic capital) is called into question.

In the rural context, the concept of strategy can be applied to various aspects of development, resource management, and community planning. Here are a few examples:

Rural Economic Development: Strategies can be developed to stimulate economic growth and improve the quality of life in rural areas. This might involve identifying and promoting local industries and businesses, attracting investment, fostering entrepreneurship, and developing infrastructure to support economic activities.

Agriculture and Natural Resource Management: Strategy plays a crucial role in agricultural development and natural resource management in rural areas. Farmers and landowners can develop strategies for crop selection, land use planning, irrigation, pest control, and sustainable farming practices. Additionally, strategies can be devised for conserving and managing natural resources such as forests, water bodies, and wildlife.

Rural Healthcare: Developing strategies to address healthcare challenges in rural areas is essential. This could involve improving access to healthcare facilities, attracting medical professionals, implementing telemedicine initiatives, and promoting preventive healthcare measures.

Rural Education: Strategies can be formulated to enhance educational opportunities in rural communities. This might include establishing schools, improving access to quality education, integrating technology in classrooms, providing vocational training, and creating partnerships with educational institutions or organizations.

Tourism and Cultural Heritage: Rural areas often possess unique cultural heritage and natural attractions that can be leveraged for tourism development. Strategies can be developed to promote sustainable tourism, preserve cultural sites, enhance visitor experiences, and generate economic opportunities for local communities.

Community Development and Governance: Strategies can be employed to foster community participation, social cohesion, and effective governance in rural areas. This might involve engaging stakeholders, facilitating community-driven initiatives, establishing local governance structures, and promoting collaboration among different sectors of the community.

These are just a few examples of how the concept of strategy can be applied in the rural context. Strategies should be tailored to the specific needs, resources, and challenges of each rural area, considering the aspirations and priorities of the local community.

Four aspects are relevant for the formulation of a strategy:

1. that the facts are observable

2. Locating the problem

3. How to establish a conflict strategy

3.1 Delimit the territory

3.2 The role of the social actors in that territory

3.3 Knowing the norms and traditions of social actors

3.4 Identifying the issues and power relations

3.5 Describing the interactions between individuals

3.6 To observe who has the upper hand in these interactions.

3.7 From this, the advantage is established or strengthened, which means the conflict strategy.

4. How the phases and timing of a strategy can be designed.

Local economic development

Local economic development is characterised by the efficient utilisation of local economic potential, which is facilitated by the proper functioning of institutions and regulatory mechanisms in the local area. The form of productive organisation, family structures and local traditions, the social and cultural structure, and the codes of conduct of the population condition the processes of local development, favour or limit the economic dynamics and, ultimately, determine the specific path of development at the micro level. The process of local economic development is a process that integrates the social with the economic from two points of view: first, because cultural and social processes are used as means to enhance production and productivity; second, because the investment of economic resources itself is carried out with the conviction of solving local problems that affect businesses and the local economy, but also community organisational action.

According to ILPES (1998), local development can be defined as that process that reactivates the economy and dynamizes local society, which, through the efficient use of the endogenous resources existing in each area, is capable of stimulating its economic growth, creating employment and improving the quality of life of the local community.

Following other authors, local development could also be defined as "a process by which local government establishes initiatives, promotes economic and social activities and connects them with social subjects in joint projects or by encouraging them in order to create new jobs and regenerate the socio-economic structure of the area" (ILPES, 1998).

These definitions clearly show the importance of local spaces in promoting the development of a region or a nation. However, some authors highlight the relevance of global processes in rural spaces. In this sense, Teubal (2001) and Pérez (2001) analyse the influence of globalisation processes on the agrarian and agro-food problems of Latin America and the way in which they affect what has been called the "new rurality", considering the transformations that have taken place in the agricultural sector and the world agro-food system, and their impact on the Latin American rural environment.

According to the analysis of the authors, globalisation has gained important spaces in the rural world, the expansion of capital and the global agro-food system are very clear examples of these advances. The integration of agricultural activities with the processing sector is causing migratory movements to the big cities; peasants, small and medium producers are being forced to leave the countryside because they cannot compete with a new generation of producers who have the means of production and who are often the owners of the agro-industrial sector, not to mention the fact that financial resources and state policies are oriented towards promoting and protecting this phenomenon that has caused globalisation.

These points attempt to take a broad view of the other side of the accentuated process of globalisation, a process in which many peripheral countries are currently involved. The changes that took place in the 1970s set the tone with a change in the strategy of the United States in relation to trade in agricultural products (expansion of cereal exports), and in response to this phenomenon (external food dependence), Third World countries promoted a series of projects aimed at food self-sufficiency.

In the 1980s, because of the Uruguay Round, North American pretensions were consolidated, with a series of deregulations of the industrial sector and a dismantling of support programmes for the agricultural sector. Large transnational agribusiness corporations were a major factor in establishing policies that influenced foreign trade, with many of these firms controlling the global food trade.

In the 1990s, to avoid the collapse of Latin American economies, international agencies promoted non-traditional exports, but these policies were really aimed at trade liberalisation and structural adjustments.

These changes, aimed at stimulating local economies, gave rise to environmental problems; these environmental problems caused health costs for the farmer and the allocation of financial and economic resources was regressive, i.e., the policies aimed at promoting agricultural activity were insufficient and misdirected.

This rearrangement of local economies under the influences of the global agri-food system led to a crisis in the domestic markets of these economies with a growing dependence on imports. Crops with "comparative" advantages were promoted to alleviate this situation but what was being done was to promote other markets. Once the markets for agricultural products and their processing were controlled, the aim was to control the markets for inputs and technology, and this was successfully achieved.

There is no doubt that globalisation is working against social equity, with transnational agro-industrial corporations increasingly taking advantage of the means of production in the rural world, transforming the traditional agricultural social structure into a capitalist one, generating what is currently called the "new rurality".

Evidently, the positive effects of both the models developed in the past and the current one, driven by the phenomenon of globalisation, do not reach the peasant and indigenous communities of Latin America. However, authors such as Linck (2001), for example, are committed to the positive effects of globalisation.

The establishment of a local development model has its advantages and disadvantages. Disadvantage, insofar as it simplifies the complexity of a process with multiple dimensions. Advantage, because it is necessary to have a methodological framework to set the reference guidelines for local development policies. In other words, what are the central components of a local development policy?

In his analysis, Linck (2001) stresses that the old way of thinking about increasing and increasing food production and offering it at low cost is evolving; this trend is closely linked to input and equipment suppliers and agro-industry. The evolution of markets and the multipolar configuration of urban systems have matured. Today, the location and prosperity of rural areas depend on the proximity of agro-industry and dynamic markets. Rural spaces located in inaccessible regions seem to be losing the advantages of these interactions with the city.

Due to these dynamics of rural space, new functions of the rural have emerged, the boundary between urban and rural is disappearing, creating a multipolar territorial organisation with an orientation towards integrality and a territorial recomposition for social actors. These trends obviously lead to new orientations in public policies, as well as to the design and enactment of laws aimed at promoting, regulating, and protecting this new rurality.

This reorganisation of the rural space implies new ways of thinking in the environmental, social, cultural and economic spheres, making it necessary to propose new competitive approaches to deal with the interactions between the city and its surrounding rural areas. This competitive approach in the new rurality involves recognising the origin of foodstuffs, being sure that the production process intrinsic to this product was carried out under heritage values, where an additional cost for this environmental, aesthetic or cultural service is well worth paying.

This brief overview of old and new trends in favour of the development of rural areas is a critique of the little impact they have had on rural society and especially on the peasant and indigenous sector.

In this sense, the process of local development should be characterised by the efficient use of the local economic potential, which should be facilitated by the adequate functioning of institutions as mechanisms of territorial regulation. The form of productive organisation, the peasant and indigenous domestic units, local traditions and the population's codes of conduct condition the processes of local development, favour or limit the economic dynamics and, in short, determine the specific path of regional development. Delgado Barrios (2003) and González et al. (2004) stress that a relevant element in a process of local economic development is the construction of social networks of community participation.

The process of local economic development must be seen from a multidimensional perspective, in which the four aspects of this perspective are integrated, as FAO (1999) aptly describes them.

The environmental element: Agriculture, land use and other functions currently attributed to rural areas can have an impact on the environment for better or worse. This vision identifies opportunities to maximise the relationship of agricultural activity with the biophysical properties of the natural environment.

☐ The multifunctional character of agriculture and land is used less when natural resources are more abundant and cultivated ecosystems are resilient.

The economic element: Agriculture remains an important force in sustaining activity and the development of the economy. Assessing the various economic functions requires weighing their short-, medium- and long-term benefits. Decisive factors in the economic function include the complexity and maturity of market development and the level of institutional evolution.

☐ The multifunctional character of agriculture and land is most applicable in the presence of well-functioning structures associated with the market economy, which implies a strong parallel performance of public institutions and decision-making procedures.

The political element: The role of the state is relevant in shaping the structures to drive local economic development.

☐ Castells (1999) points out that state intervention plays a relevant role in the delay or acceleration of technological modernisation and that the state acts in order to maintain control over its society. If the state perceives that by technologically modernising its society it may lose control over it, then it will avoid modernisation processes in its society and vice versa.

The social element: To sustain agro-ecology and improve the quality of life in the rural sector, the conservation and dynamism of rural communities are essential. On the other hand, it is critical for the future of today's rural communities to build on local knowledge and to link local and foreign expertise, information, and advisory resources. Social viability includes the preservation of cultural heritage.

☐ The multifunctional character of agriculture and land can be optimal when communication between stakeholders at all levels is direct and transparent.

These elements described above, as well as others that stand out and will be addressed later, are territory, local knowledge, the role of peasant households, the role of indigenous households, relational dynamics and mental models, and the role of the local community.

Territorial development

The persistence of marginalisation in the countryside, the concentration of the most extreme forms of poverty in rural areas and the growing inequality in the distribution of rural incomes continue to be very worrying results of the often-costly efforts undertaken to combat rural poverty and inequality in Latin America through rural development initiatives. This widespread failure calls for the exploration of alternative approaches to rural development that are more likely to succeed. One such alternative deserves special attention, which aims to: (1) project the added value of underutilised local resources to their maximum potential, (2) integrate rural and urban activities into a single territorial dimension, focusing on regional economic projects, and (3) incorporate the rural poor into the employment and investment opportunities generated by local growth (Janvry and Sadoulet, 2004).

Janvry and Sadoulet (2004), mention a set of dimensions for adopting a territorial approach:

Dimension 1: Definition of the region

According to the territorial approach to rural development, regions can be defined in various ways and are classified into the following four types:

☐ Municipality, for the purpose of local government. Municipalities can be effective in the provision of public goods and services at the local level but are generally too small for the administration of successful economic projects. However, when municipalities are large, they can serve as economic units for regional development.

☐ Ad-hoc association of municipalities for special projects (e.g., watershed management or the provision of a certain public service).

☐ Regions as larger administrative units: sub-national governments at state level.

☐ Regions, as functional economic units: natural economic unit with shared comparative advantages, common pool of diversified employment or unit of social capital. These regions can be functionally defined by organisations such as a development bank (such as the Banco do Nordeste for agro-industrial development, BANDES and the Micro financings for small and medium entrepreneurs in Venezuela), a cooperative (e.g., the one used for non-traditional exports in Guatemala) or a processing centre (such as the dairy production systems in Peru and Brazil). For these regions, the linkages between rural areas and urban centres are fundamental.

The authors suggest three administrative levels for territorial development:

☐ National and state level, if it is a federative system of government.

☐ Regional level: sub-national administrative unit, coalition of municipalities or functional economic unit.

☐ Local level: municipality

Dimension 2: Institutional transformation of the region

Element 1: Strengthen and modernise local government capacity

☐ Increased economic capacity: Fiscal and financial decentralisation (credit capacity).

☐ Improved administrative capacity and accountability.

☐ Capacity to deliver efficient and high quality basic services.

Element 2: Strengthening the capacity of local organisations (social, economic and political capital)

□ Strengthening civil society and private sector representative organisations

Element 3: Form institutions whose purpose is to plan and formulate regional and local development projects.

□ Create institutions for consultation, coordination and cooperation between the public, private and civil society sectors, especially regional and local development councils.

□ Regional strategic planning capacity: conceptualisation and operationalisation of a strategic vision for the region, with broad participation of public, civil and private sector bodies (regional development agency). Regional and local development project definitions.

□ Capacity of local universities for innovation, training and technical assistance.

□ Regional institutions to promote the region (chambers of commerce and industry, product labelling, quality certification, regional image building [with a specialised branding firm] and advertising).

□ Coordination with national infrastructure and competitiveness promotion programmes.

Dimension 3: Productive transformation of the region

Element 1: Regional infrastructure and financial development projects (state-region contracts)

☐ Public investments in infrastructure, particularly aimed at linking the region to dynamic national and international markets.

☐ Development of local and regional financial institutions

Element 2: Promoting the competitiveness of the region and local entrepreneurs (regionally driven development projects)

☐ Investments in entrepreneurial skills training, technical assistance and public business incubators.

☐ Subsidies to investments that generate positive local externalities (decentralisation, agglomeration) through grants and/or tax exemptions.

☐ Support for investments in the region's comparative advantages: Promote "new agriculture" (local production systems for high-value crops and animal products (dairy, cheese), quality, own labelling, value added through processing, contracts with supermarkets and agro-industries, food security for exports).

☐ Promote the rural non-farm economy: linkage with activities related to agriculture, decentralisation of manufacturing. New services (environmental services, tourism, ecotourism, services for retired people) and proximity economy (local transport, subcontracting).

□ Use transfers and remittances as a source of financing and investment (capitalisation of local financial institutions).

Dimension 4: Social transformation of the region

Rural development programme (social and productive expenditure) supporting social inclusion of the poor

□ Improve the asset position of the rural poor: Access to land: redistributive land reform and land purchase subsidies, Human capital formation: conditional cash transfer programmes for education and health (Progresa and Oportunidades in Mexico, Bolsa Escola in Brazil, Barrio Adentro in Venezuela) and Social capital formation: promoting membership in organisations.

□ Combat the reproduction and deepening of social inequalities to ensure that the benefits of local and regional development are shared by all.

□ Safety net programmes that support risk-taking by the poor.

Dimension 5: Implementation of territorial comprehensive development as a national strategy: Accountability and learning

□ Audit and impact analysis for accountability.

□ Results-based management for participatory learning and just-in-time impact analysis and Ensuring continuity beyond the political cycle and initial leadership (Cajamarca, Cuatro

Pinos, Guatemala): importance of broad social participation in the region and national and international visibility beyond the regional level.

How to avoid bottlenecks

There have been many scattered attempts at territorial approaches to rural development. The lessons learned from these experiences provide a record of pitfalls and bottlenecks to be avoided. These, of course, are specific to each situation and therefore difficult to generalise. However, several pitfalls can be mentioned that help to prevent the repetition of costly mistakes.

1. Lack of sufficient managerial capacity at the local level. The decentralisation that is part of the territorial approach implies the transfer to local governments of functions that were previously assumed by a specialised central bureaucratic apparatus. Local administration may not be ready to take on such functions. However, Bolivia's experience revealed that this was not a major limiting factor for municipal administration of social expenditures (Janvry and Sadoulet, 2004). However, the observed bias away from productive projects may reflect a lack of management capacity for more complex income-generating projects. The change of charismatic political leaders in the administration may also become a problem.

Lack of financial capacity and sustainability at the local level beyond the flow of transfers. In most cases, decentralisation has been the transfer of administrative functions without fiscal decentralisation. Half decentralisation makes local decision-making entirely dependent on state and central government allocations. For this reason, the deepening of fiscal reforms is a necessary element in the implementation of a territorial approach.

3. Shortage of funds to implement projects. In the Cajamarca experience, coordination and planning were effectively carried out at the regional level. However, decentralisation was not supported by the national government, which meant that funds were not available to implement regional projects. One way to overcome this difficulty would be to implement a Region Driven Development (DIR) approach, like the proven Community Driven Development (CDD) approach.

4. Lack of a mid-level administrative structure. Most Latin American countries have central (federal), state and municipal levels of government. Since municipalities are too small, and states too large, to handle regional economic projects, there is a need for a systematic mid-level administrative level that corresponds to the concept of territory for the purposes of regional projects. Mexico employs 140 DDRs (Distritos de Desarrollo Rural) as units at a medium level above the

municipal level, together with a rural development council at the district level (as specified in the Ley de Desarrollo Rural Sostenible). However, these may also be too small to implement economically important projects. Brazil, on the other hand, uses coalitions of municipalities and their corresponding territorial development councils. Generally speaking, Latin America shows a great lack of middle-level administrative structures.

5. Excessive decentralisation has led to atomisation and loss of economies of scale in economic projects. This has been the case in the Bolivian experience. A possible solution to this difficulty is the regrouping of municipalities into local coalitions and the search for coordination of investments at this level.

6. Complementation with sector-wide approaches. In some cases, sector-wide approaches to rural development work well. This was the case in Asia's Green Revolution, where property rights, institutions and markets helped support the adoption of new technological alternatives, and where agro-ecological conditions were favourable. When all these conditions are not met, a territorial approach offers an alternative to identify the set of constraints that stand in the way of adopting new technologies and to design these technologies in a participatory way, adapting them to the

heterogeneity of local needs. This is the approach taken by the CGIAR Challenge Programme for Sub-Saharan Africa, which seeks to promote technological change where it has previously failed.

7. Deep inequalities at the local level that allow local elites to reap the benefits. Much has been said about the dangers of decentralisation, as local elites seize control of local resources for their own benefit. Empirical studies on Asia tend to show that regressive allocations are more of a problem between the central state and regions than between regions and municipalities (Janvry and Sadoulet [2004] in the case of India). Nevertheless, the extreme levels of inequality at the local level in Latin America indicate the need to address the issue of how social inequalities are reproduced as a condition for the success of territorial approaches.

8. Lack of interest of urban areas in coordinating investments with rural areas. A systematic bias towards the urban and formal sectors in policy has been a marked feature of the ISI (Import Substitution Industrialisation) model, which has led to the current paradox of resource under-utilisation. However, rural areas can mobilise underutilised resources through a process of coordination and planning that is in the interest of urban residents. This includes access to cheap and reliable labour (as in the case of Italian industrial districts) for

the decentralisation of economic activity and the supply of raw materials to urban industries, as well as the provision of water, recreation and environmental services for consumers. Linking rural and urban areas around regional development requires clear identification and promotion of the benefits to be gained by the parties.

9. Lack of producer organisations. The social fund model does not produce sustained benefits for the poor if they lack representation and bargaining power (Janvry and Sadoulet 2004). This calls for the promotion of representative organisations of these groups. Strengthening producer organisations has been an important dimension of regional development efforts promoted by the World Bank (see for example, Janvry and Sadoulet 2004).

10. The need to sustain activities beyond the local political period. Especially at the local level, elected officials are often subject to non-renewable and very short terms of office (two years and no right to re-election in Mexico, for example), which implies major discontinuities in local initiatives. This is one of the reasons why local development councils (which operate in Mexico, Brazil and Uruguay) offer the possibility of continuity beyond political cycles, with the risk of creating parallel administrative structures that have not been popularly elected.

11. The need for a high-impact approach. Territorial investments need to reach a scale large enough to generate the necessary spill-over effects to unleash local endogenous growth. This is the idea behind the organisation of local clusters of small and medium-sized enterprises in Brazil. This underlines the need to adopt a high-thrust approach. The commitment to this approach must therefore be such that it can mobilise sufficient funds to support projects of such a magnitude that they trigger productivity gains from local spill-over effects. In general terms the EU LEADER project has not been able to achieve these scale effects due to overly dispersed small-scale territorial initiatives.

Other authors such as Méndez Espinoza (2005), point out that the territory in each rural development process is a social construction, and not an "objectively existing" space that can be delimited by a purely technical ex ante exercise by virtue of one or another variable or set of physical or economic variables. The operational definition of territory is purely instrumental, i.e., functional to the objectives and scope of the project proposed by the agents of rural territorial development processes. For the Inter-American Institute for Cooperation on Agriculture (Méndez Espinoza, 2005), rural territories are defined as geographic spaces whose cohesion derives from a specific social fabric, a particular natural resource base, institutions and forms of organisation, and certain forms of production, exchange, and income distribution.

In this sense, I believe it is necessary to highlight some aspects of IICA's proposal on the territorial approach to sustainable rural development. Sepulveda et al. (2003) present the fundamentals of the proposed model, emphasising its holistic nature and its consistency with sustainable rural development approaches. They also point out its relevance as a reference framework for promoting social and territorial cohesion.

The proposed model is based on several elements, including the definition of territory and the need to adopt a country vision. In this sense, the main objective for the harmonious achievement of development goals, within the framework of a national territorial vision, must be the definition of a vision of the country, whose fundamental aspiration is to offer prosperity to the greatest possible part of the rural population, a goal that can only be achieved by promoting equity, productive competitiveness, sustainable management of the environment, political stability, and democratic governance. When talking about prosperity, the territorial approach has as indisputable references, the overcoming of rural poverty and the food security of the rural population.

This model responds to the different events that have taken place around the world, aimed at reducing poverty and hunger and promoting social equity, and constitutes an alternative to conventional approaches to rural development. For the present work, the territory will be a social construction that derives from a historical process and a cultural process where the interactions of the social subjects shape it.

Territorial development according to IICA

IICA highlights the following elements:

1. Reconstructing the concept of the rural

☐ Rurality then becomes strategic in the construction of a sustainable development model, harmonious in its relationship with the natural resource base, and economically, politically and socially viable.

2. The shift from an agricultural economy to a territorial economy

☐ This economy of the territory is shaped by the natural resource base of the territory (natural capital); the productive activities and economic structure that are developed from this natural resource base (economic, physical and financial capital); the demographic dynamics and social relations that accompany the shaping of the economic structure; and the institutional processes that lead to these social relations (human capital and social capital). Therefore, the importance of natural capital, human capital, social capital, physical capital and financial capital as basic supports of the economy of rural territories is recognised; that is, it is based on a broad vision of capital, in which what is important is not only economic, but also social, economic, physical and financial.

3. Rescuing the territorial and local rural economy in growth strategies

☐ Rural territories are economic units in which different types of exchange are practised: internally with a local economy; and externally with an export market that includes other territories or localities, other regional or national spaces and the international economy. The dynamics established by these activities determine the possibilities for economic growth and wealth generation.

4. Environmental management and the development of markets for environmental services

☐ Environmental services play an economic role that has been ignored and excluded from the production functions of the rural territory, but which can be incorporated in different ways - currently incipient, but surely solid in the not too distant future - into local development models. The sustainable management of natural resources, ecotourism and rural tourism are some examples of this new type of activities, which are already showing interesting results in many initiatives throughout the continent.

5. The shift from private competitiveness to territorial competitiveness

☐ The competitiveness of firms contributes to generate private rents and these determine private wealth; the competitiveness of the territory contributes to generate social rents and these contribute to form the social wealth of the territory.

☐ Therefore, a territory is competitive when it combines a model that, while guaranteeing high private profitability to the firms that are located there (private wealth), also guarantees high social profitability to the population that makes it up. In other words, a territory will be competitive when firms and communities perceive it as attractive to locate or stay in it.

6. Territorial planning as a complement to decentralisation

☐ Decentralisation has led to deconcentrated administration, but not necessarily to a change in the political responsibilities of the territories, in line with the structural adjustments that the continent is undergoing

7. Cooperation and shared responsibility as a complement to participation and as key elements for the integration of top-down and bottom-up approaches.

☐ Local cooperation goes beyond participation. It is a broader form of public-private relationship; it relies on the autonomy of communities, their institutions, organisations and entrepreneurs, and implies a rethinking of the dynamics, initiatives and processes of development management.

☐ Cooperation is based on the recognition of the social actors present in a given territory and leads to self-management and shared responsibility as expressions of the collective will to establish their own rules of the game, commitments and organisational forms, and to have, in this way, a more certain possibility of empowerment.

☐ From this coincidence arises a new state-society relationship, with new contractual models and new tasks for the state and private agents.

8. Coordination between macro, sectoral and local policies

☐ If a new approach to agricultural and rural development is to make an effective contribution to reducing poverty and food insecurity, it must involve all actors in local and regional development in the current economic production model.

☐ Such an approach, however, requires the establishment of integrated policies, as opposed to the predominance of a sectoral approach. This articulation finds in the rural territory its natural setting and in the communities themselves, entrepreneurs and authorities, the ideal agents to oversee its management.

9. Knowledge management for rural development

□ A knowledge management system for rural development can fulfil such functions as:

a) To serve as a space for experimenting with new practices.

b) To be a training scenario.

c) Facilitate articulation with key partners.

d) To be a mechanism to attract opportunities.

It is stressed that these elements must be framed in a broader scenario where multidimensionality, temporality and intergenerationality, multisectoriality, the articulation of a territorial economy and the search for greater institutional coincidence operate.

For Méndez Espinoza (2005) it is also important to specify, among other elements, the transcendental role played by cultural characteristics in the conception of territory, through which phenomena of socialisation of space are projected and identified, the result of which is called territory. Consequently, any process that is established in contravention of social and/or natural patterns in each geographical area, and that detaches and destroys the principles of spatial unity and social cohesion, can be identified as a factor that contributes to the disintegration of such unity insofar as it stimulates and triggers phenomena of deterritorialization or territorial disarticulation.

For the present work, because of the revision of the concept, coinciding with Méndez Espinoza (2005), territory is taken up again as a social construction, derived from its history, its culture, and the identity processes of its inhabitants, being a dynamic and open space.

Territorial competitiveness

A relevant aspect derived from the territorial approach is territorial competitiveness, a concept that has been developed by Canzanelli (2004) and Portilla Rodríguez (2003).

Canzanelli (2004), intends to teach an alternative way of combating poverty, through local development policies, based on the endogenous potential of a territory, an aspect that is in an experimental phase and that has been initiated in some developing countries. The theories and models of territorial development of endogenous potential have proven their validity in many developed countries, as a third way to development in the face of Keynesian policies on the one hand and the free market game on the other. On the one hand, the author analyzes the concept of endogenous potential and its role in territorial development, arguing that endogenous factors contribute to the process of capital accumulation, generating external and internal economies of scale, economies of agglomeration and diversity, which reduce overhead and transaction costs and favour economies of diversity. The problem, in many cases of weak areas, is that it is difficult to identify the potential that leads a territory to qualitative and quantitative growth.

The endogenous potential of a territory is the set of resources of different nature that can be exploited to build a sustainable and competitive development. Every territory, even the most marginal ones such as the Sahara desert or the Siberian savannah, has at least one resource that can be exploited for its own development. In the poorest areas, this type of resource is very often the only one to count on for development, since it is difficult for external investments to arrive, due to lack of convenience (Canzanelli, 2004).

According to Canzanelli (2004), each territory is articulated according to its own character, its own history, its culture, etc. In this sense, local economies do not passively adapt to national or international processes and transformations, but their adjustment is closely related to an economic, political, social and cultural identity that has been defined over time. For this reason, development policies must always consider the particularities and specificities of the territory.

The theory of endogenous development, Canzanelli (2004), considers capital accumulation and technological progress as key factors in economic growth. Since economic development occurs as a consequence of the processes that determine capital accumulation, such as the creation and diffusion of innovations in the productive system, the flexible organization of production, this theory identifies a self-sustaining development path by arguing that endogenous factors contribute to the process of capital accumulation, generating economies, external and internal, of scale, economies of agglomeration and diversity, which reduce general costs and transaction costs and favor economies of diversity. There is no doubt that the processes of growth and structural change in economies occur because of the introduction of innovations in the productive system through investment decisions. However, the economic effects of innovations depend on how they are diffused in the productive fabric and on the technological strategy of companies in their struggle to maintain or improve the results of their activity. However, the processes of diffusion of innovations and knowledge are conditioned by the environment, the territory (system of companies, institutions, economic and social actors) in which companies make their investment decisions. This environment is made up of fundamentally endogenous factors, which are different territory by territory, characterize and distinguish them, making the development trajectories of each of them specific, and multiplying (through differentiation) the supply of products and services in the global market. Consequently, as Canzanelli (2004) points out, "creative regional growth" or the creation of a territorial environment that stimulates innovation in the productive and business fabric are crucial aspects in the design of development strategies.

Social subjects in the rural context

In a framework of analysis for the elaboration of strategies for local development, the role played by social actors is relevant, especially peasants and indigenous people with their respective domestic units. In this sense, Sepúlveda et al. (2003) analyzes the importance of social subjects in the construction of their territories, from which the following is derived:

Social subjects are conceived as population groups with interests, conditions and characteristics that identify them as such. Even when there are self-interests and initiatives that may motivate antagonism among actors, they also have the potential to cooperate and manage joint actions, with other actors or with public or private institutions, for the common good of rural society. Social actors may be individuals, formal and informal organizations, or institutions, insofar as the plans and strategies of some coincide, at a given moment, with those of others.

A single action of social subjects constitutes their maximum capital. It is social capital, and this capital is nourished by the energy of relationships, networks and social ties, which serve to satisfy specific purposes of survival, reproduction or improvement of living conditions.

The generation, in specific territories, of new social and cultural contracts capable of orienting the interaction between human populations and natural resources towards sustainability has profound ethical (society puts individual interest before the collective well-being of the present and the future) and institutional implications. The territorial approach provides an opportunity to understand social and cultural diversity as a strength that can be exploited to increase the level of development management in its various forms, not only at the local but also at the national level. The concept of differentiated social policies has been used by IICA to refer to the strategic potential of rural youth, rural women and indigenous peoples who, because of their particular conditions, are key to social change, sustainability and equity in rural territories in general. For the purposes of this document, the social subjects will be analyzed separately due to their specificities and differences; in the first part we will deal with the peasant and his household unit, then we will deal with the indigenous person and his household unit.

The peasant organization, the peasant and his household unit

Farmers' organization

When we talk about farmer organization, we imagine a group of people gathered around a goal. On the other hand, when we speak of a business organization, we imagine a set of relationships, task assignment, efficiency, and productivity. There are marked differences in each type of organization; however, there is always an attempt to impose the business organization scheme on farmer organizations without considering that the relationships between individuals take place under different conditions.

Marx's Theory of Value explains how these profits are obtained, which are basically the relationship between the value of the product minus the cost of producing it; but additionally, there is a surplus labor, which is the extra work done by the worker that is not paid, and which is called surplus value.

Differences between a farmer organization and a business organization

Business Organization	Farmer Organization
➢ Organizational conflicts are between the owner and the workers.	➢ Conflicts occur in the environment of the organization and are caused by a power relationship.
➢ The owner owns all the means of production.	➢ Each member of the organization is both owner and worker, i.e., the workers own the means of production.
➢ The knowledge to operate is in the managers.	➢ The knowledge to operate is in each member of the organization.
➢ The organization has the resources to operate.	➢ They require a political component to obtain resources.

Today, society has imposed norms at all levels of the economic, social, political, environmental, and even cultural spheres, under this context a new world order has emerged, which has led the economies of peripheral countries to reorient their policies to be able to position themselves in these scenarios.

In this sense, governments and their policies are oriented to compete under very unequal conditions, as is the case, for example, of subsidies in the central countries, which fully protect the farmer. This is not the case in peripheral countries where farmers do not have any type of subsidy under the same terms as in the central countries, causing small and medium farmers to be unable to compete and consequently they are absorbed by large farmers, generating a change of subsistence strategy in small and medium producers, turning them into just another wage-earner.

In this context, where there is a power relationship between the central countries and the peripheral countries, the latter have reformed their legal structure so that the small farmer or peasant disappears.

It should be noted that the few remaining farmers in these countries who try to organize themselves are literally forced to operate under competitive schemes, without considering that these social subjects have a value structure different from that existing in a business-type organization. It is important to point out that since the 1960's an attempt was made to impose the concept of the North American family farm, this phenomenon took hold and became the productive unit model of a certain ideological current that sought to modernize agriculture through agrarian reform and the colonization of new lands. It was conceived as the type of agrarian enterprise most consistent with an accelerated rate of adoption of technical changes in agriculture.

It is the case that the authorities responsible for conducting agricultural policies in the peripheral countries try to manage these peasant organizations as business organizations, predisposing in advance the failure of any development program aimed at these social subjects. In this aspect, the subjects have evolved in terms of organization where the power relationship has prevailed as a way of achieving their objectives and obtaining resources for their sustainability.

An approach to the concept of peasant

The elaboration of a current concept of peasant that is valid for the study of Latin American peasant forms encounters many difficulties. The diversity of criteria used, the insufficient empirical data on the diversity of forms and the tendency to instrumentalize them in terms of various ideological objectives are some important factors that hinder the achievement of this task, aspects that coincide with those pointed out by Méndez Espinoza (2005). According to Simonde de Sismondi, the peasant is any farmer who lives from the products of the plot of land he cultivates, where the product can be destined primarily for his own consumption, or for sale, the labor force can be his own and family, but can be completed with the help of servants or servants, slaves, or day laborers hired by the day. In the same sense of small farmer of a plot of land on whose products he lives (whether or not he pays rents or taxes in labor, kind or money, whether or not the product is destined to the market; whether he is free, a serf of a landowner or a taxpayer of a state), the concept of peasant is used by J. Stuart Mill, Kautski, Marx, Hertz, David, Lenin, Luxemburg, Childe and in general the great majority of social scientists in the world (Méndez Espinoza, 2005).

Hernández (n/d) points out that the peasant has been conceived in relation to an economy, a culture or a social class, according to different conceptual traditions. The classical authors of Marxism, such as Marx and Lenin, conceive the peasant as a social class oppressed and exploited by the pre-capitalist society, privileging the analysis of classes and their subordinate position. But from Chayanov onwards, a dominant tendency arises in conceiving the peasants as belonging to a specific and singular economy, coexisting in a capitalist economic system. The French historian D. Thorner (1979), speaks of a peasant economy characterized fundamentally by producing for exchange, a feature that distinguishes them from tribal societies. The anthropologist R. Firth conceives of peasants as "a system of small producers, with simple technology and equipment, who often depend primarily for their subsistence on what they produce themselves".

There seems to be substantial agreement in locating peasants as a phenomenon as distinct from primitive farmers. What seems to be implied in the classical definitions of Kroeber and Redfield is that peasants constitute partial societies with partial cultures and are under the structural dependence of cities (Kroeber, 1948 and Redfield, 1956 cited by Archetti, 1978).

Another approach is pointed out by Wolf, who says that peasants are agricultural producers (different from fishermen, artisans, etc.), that they have control of the land and that their production is oriented towards subsistence (Archetti, 1978). What is common to all these approaches is the scientific search for a general model that tries to isolate those elements that are common to peasant societies and peasants in general. There is nothing wrong with definitions insofar as they allow us to avoid repetitions by fixing those characteristics that are repeated in different times and spaces. "Peasant" as a definition, as a type, as a generalization falls somehow in the middle of a definition of worker taken in its most general form and another definition of worker that specifies precise historical and social conditions. The worker under certain conditions can be subsumed under the general definition but is at the same time something else (Archetti, 1978).

For Bartra (1998), the peasant may have land and even a modest capital, he sells or eats what he harvests and if at times he hires day laborers, at others he sells himself for a day's wage. The peasant is a bit like the landowner, like the bourgeois and like the proletariat. He is a polymorphous phantom defined by his intricate complexity. Peasants are all of them, but none is the "peasant", a class without uniform is difficult to capture, sometimes it appears in the photo, but we do not know which one it is: if the Purhépecha indigenous just reintegrated to his community, the northern man in boots and tall hat looking at the camera, the barefoot Mixe who carries firewood among the vertiginous hills or the young man in tennis shoes and computer who downloads from the Internet the latest coffee quotations.

For the present document an approximation to the conceptual construction of the peasant is oriented to the fact that he is a being who is positioned in a social phenomenal world, he is in the historical, ethical, folkloric, and religious context and can hardly be definable, not even indefinable, due to the multiplicity of roles he fulfills in today's society. Today's peasant is a mixture of past, present and future, and this affirmation is the key to his social reproduction.

The peasant household unit (UDC)

According to Deere and Janvry (1992), what distinguishes the peasant household unit from other household units (such as the household in advanced capitalism) is that the household is both a unit of direct production and a unit of family labor force reproduction on a daily and generational basis. At a given moment in time, the capital of family labor in relation to the household's access to the means of production is reflected in the division of labor by dry and age incorporating into the household labor process. The household labor force is either used in the household production process or sold as wage labor in the labor market where it participates in what is called the wage labor production process. A continuous spectrum of combinations can be identified between the two pure extreme types of households: the purely agriculturalist and the purely proletarian. Household labor engaged in home production generates a gross product that is retained as use-value by the household for home consumption or sold on the market as a commodity (the circulation process). Here, again, a continuum can be identified between pure subsistence household production with no marketable surplus and the purely commercial estate that is producing exclusively for the market.

Deere and Janvry (1992) mention that there are four key processes identified that characterize the organization of the peasant household unit - the household production process, the wage labor production process, the circulation process and the reproduction-differentiation process.

For Chayanov, the CDUs are units that produce in not very extensive areas and lacking appropriate technology; in which the specialized cultivation tasks sometimes demand an exceptional accumulation of labor mass in very short periods, therefore they find the need to hire labor force, since the family one is not enough; while in other periods of the agricultural year that can be very long, agriculture does not find where to employ the peasant labor force. The volume of activity of the work force is therefore adjusted to the size of these factors; in view of this, the labor force of the family that exploits the unit, not finding employment in the domestic exploitation, turns to other non-agricultural activities, producing only the unit with the minimum availability of its means of production (Méndez Espinoza, 2005).

The Marxist-Chayanov analysis is in a historical context where the rural population was the majority, and for both the main element of organization of the domestic unit was the availability of family labor force, under the practice of a mercantile economy and where the fruits of labor are directed to the subsistence of the CDU. Both cite the limits of property (smallholdings), as well as of the available factors, where their disappearance was a way for the development of agriculture according to the analysis of the former. For the latter, the diversification of the labor force in extra-industrial activities was already a fact, given the seasonality of agricultural production, and a strategy that has allowed its permanence in the current context, in the face of an adverse context such as that cited by Marx of the development of the social productive forces of labor, social concentration of capital and the progressive application of science (Méndez Espinoza, 2005).

The concept of domestic unit, according to Oliveira and Salles (1989) cited by Méndez Espinoza (2005), refers to an organization structured based on networks of social relations established between individuals, whether or not united by kinship ties, who share a residence and organize daily reproduction in common. For Méndez Espinoza (2005), it is necessary to integrate into the reproduction dynamics of these groups according to the context.

Indigenous and indigenous organization

The indigenous organization

Indigenous social organization tends to be considered by experts as a primordial factor that characterizes ethnicity in indigenous peoples and communities as a collectivity. This is certainly not surprising, since it is where conceptions, values, norms, cohesion, reproduction, and self-regulation mechanisms are condensed. The organization is the basis for its own institutions and what we could call the indigenous government or political system. It is convenient, to go deeper into this topic, to conceive the indigenous social organization as a system where the political, religious-ceremonial, agrarian-environmental and natural resources, moral and normative-legal aspects are articulated and acquire a sense of a whole, of esprit de corps, as they depend on a common logic, that of complementarity (Ávila Méndez, 2002).

The indigenous organizations believe that there is a low capacity of the political system and the State to process their differentiated demands that are affirmed in their identity, such as collective rights, recognition, bilingualism and biculturalism, or the extension and restitution of community lands.

To understand the current processes involving indigenous peoples and the conflicts arising from their action in the public space, it is necessary to understand that what is commonly referred to as "indigenous movement" - in our case, we prefer the concept of "ethnic movement" - is not a meta-social expression, nor a unitary empirical object whose existence can be manifested in a self-referential abstraction. On the contrary, as Melucci points out, social movements are rather "systems of action, complex networks between the different levels and meanings of social action" (Melucci, 1999, p.12 cited by Bello, 2004). They are thus different levels that express a plurality of levels of action, at different times, with different forms of organization and leadership, as well as strategies and discourses. Unlike Touraine, Melucci places greater emphasis not on the identity of movements, the search for defining features or historicity, but on the field of relationships and meanings. In these terms, a social movement is the product of the exchanges, conflicts, and negotiations that subjects establish through networks of solidarity and the production of cultural meanings, the latter of which ultimately differentiates them from political and institutional actors (Bello, 2004).

How is indigenous collective action expressed? In various ways: as rebellion, as social outburst, as protest, but also as negotiation and participation through citizen channels and traditional representation structures. However, for part of the specialized literature, as well as for the press and common sense, conflict has become a central defining factor of indigenous collective action. The "indigenous problem" has always been spoken of as a field of complex difficulties arising from the resistance of indigenous groups to integration into national life. The indigenous conflict would be, in this sense, the result of the action of the indigenous subject, obstinate and entrenched in tradition, and refractory to receive the "offers" of modernity. From another perspective, the indigenous would be conflictive because they would pressure society and the political system with old or unattainable demands. Finally, the conflictivity of the indigenous movements would be found in the search for difference, an issue that would be contrary to modern logic if we consider that the emergence of the national state has had as its purpose the search for equality, which, despite being abstract, is universal (Bello, 2004).

The diversity of indigenous peoples is also expressed in the varied geographic spaces they occupy within the countries of the region and even beyond. Although indigenous peoples continue to be associated with rural areas, rural-urban migration and the natural growth of a population of indigenous origin in urban areas represent an increasingly evident reality. Changes in productive structures, industrial development, the expansion of urban centers, the application of massification to road infrastructure and the gradual decline of the agricultural sector are some of the major causes of indigenous migration to the cities. To these must be added local factors and dynamics, as well as family and individual motivations (Bello, 2004).

There has been a transformation of indigenous collective action, another based only on peasant and class demands, which is now expressed in the use of ethnicity and identity as a political strategy, which has encouraged new forms of group solidarity, crystallized in the constitution of an indigenous social subject that has its own ways of doing politics, with strategies and discourses sometimes detached or distant from traditional blocks. The indigenous organization and the community have also become a space for the articulation and reproduction of ethnicity, a reference point for struggles and the place where identities are recreated and organized (Albó, 2002 cited by Bello, 2004). Floriberto Díaz, Mixe anthropologist from Tlahuitoltepec and leader of the indigenous movement in Oaxaca until his death in 1995, defines community "for us, the Indians themselves" as:

☐ a territorial space, demarcated and defined by possession

☐ a common history, which circulates by word of mouth and from one generation to the next.

☐ a variant of the language of the People, from which we identify our common language

☐ an organization that defines political, cultural, social, civil, economic and religious aspects

☐ a community system for the procurement and administration of justice.

Díaz, along with many other anthropologists, insists that community is defined beyond its physical aspects or basic functions. "An indigenous community is not understood only as a set of houses with people, but people with history, past, present and future, who can not only be defined concretely, physically, but also spiritually in relation to nature as a whole."

The indigenous community has raised several discussions around its meaning. These are grouped into three questions: whether the community is fundamentally a pre-Hispanic or colonial creation; whether its development represents a human-social evolution or a specific historical dynamic; and finally, whether some representations of the indigenous community fall into specialization or mythification.

The question of their origins is one of the most controversial. Juan Pedro Viqueira gathers different positions to show which characteristics of contemporary Indian communities, considered legacies of the pre-Hispanic past, are myths that dominate the analysis of Indian communities and cloud the historical contradictions that exist within them. He criticizes above all the tendency to attribute to the indigenous community a high degree of homogeneity, economic equality, and social consensus. Viqueira cites recent studies of the Altos de Guerrero and historical works of pre-Hispanic and colonial Mexico to argue his thesis that communities with the characteristics are an ideal construction and, in general, do not exist and have not existed in the past. The problem, then, is to explain the cohesion of Indian communities and their importance as a source of ethnic identity without resorting to myths (Carlsen, 1999).

On the other hand, other authors defend the permanence of pre-Hispanic roots in Indian communities and emphasize the conservation of specifically indigenous characteristics in the social order and cosmovision of the communities. From this perspective, hierarchy, the central role of kinship relations, agrarian cycles and the link with the land, the way in which the community self-delimits itself and the construction of identities within the community have been constant since pre-Columbian times and are also features that define the community today.

The discussion of origins revolves around the relative weight assigned to continuities versus ruptures. Studies that emphasize the rupture and reconstruction of the indigenous community analyze specific political structures and external linkage mechanisms and conclude that the current form of indigenous communities is a relatively new construction. There were three main factors that definitively changed the indigenous communities and contributed to the construction of their present form. First, the epidemics that wiped out entire populations and decimated many more; the colonization process that relocated large sectors of the population to dismantle the urban centers and settle in rural communities; and secondly, the process of colonization, which led to the establishment of the indigenous communities. This colonial policy is often cited to support the hypothesis that the basic structure of Indian communities today is a creation of the Crown. The third element of radical post-conquest change comes from the imposition of political and social forms and the arrival of the Catholic Church (Carlsen, 1999 1978).

The indigenous

According to Mexican structuralism, the indigenous person is considered as such based on linguistic criteria. This is not the case for other countries with indigenous presence in which the criteria are broader, among them are the criteria of social and cultural order.

In Venezuela, according to the Law of Demarcation and Guarantee of the Habitat and Lands of Indigenous Peoples, an indigenous person is a person who recognizes him/herself and is recognized as such, originating from and belonging to a people with its own linguistic, social, cultural and economic characteristics, located in a specific region or belonging to an indigenous community.

Venezuela has an indigenous population of 724,592, which are distributed in 2,295 indigenous communities with presence in 8 States of the country. There is a need to retake the vision of a people, sustained on the one hand by the sharing of language, territory, and vision of the world, and on the other hand, by the existence of local, sectorial, and statutory authorities on which the societal and orienting articulation within them rests, and which allows basing the relationship between the national society and the indigenous people (MECD, 2003).

Mental models

Addressing the issue of the elaboration of local development strategies from the perspective of the social subject is not something new, but its implementation requires an important effort on the part of those in charge of bringing welfare to all vulnerable rural communities. I say this because since the 60's with the green revolution technicians have been taught to deposit technical knowledge to all those individuals in the countryside that in some way or another have or develop a productive activity.

It is very difficult to move away from these mental patterns, because even in university higher education the new generations of technicians continue to be taught to operate under the same mental patterns of decades ago, an aspect that Freire (1998) rightly addresses. Based on my position, I believe it is necessary to go into this aspect in detail, since it may be key to the proper use of this book. In 1983 two books on mental models were published, one written by Philip Johnson-Laird, which proposes a theory of mental models and the other edited by D. Gentner and A.L. Stevens, which focuses on the knowledge that people develop about physical phenomena and especially about mechanical and technological devices, without presenting any unified theory in this regard. Today the term mental model is increasingly used. The concept of mental model that we are going to present here is the one proposed by Johnson-Laird (1983) cited by Moreira and Greca (2002). However, to introduce it is necessary to begin with the concept of representation.

A *representation* is any notation, sign, or set of symbols that represents something that is typically some aspect of the external world or of our inner world (i.e., our imagination) in its absence. The word doll or a drawing of a doll are external representations that allow us to evoke the object doll in its absence. Mental representations are internal representations. They are ways of "re-presenting" internally (i.e., mentally), of re-presenting in our minds the external world.

A distinction can be made between analogical and propositional mental representations. The visual image is the prototypical analogical representation, but there are others such as auditory, olfactory or tactile ones. The perfume of a rose can be evoked through an olfactory image, which would mean that it would be internally represented by an olfactory image in our minds as well. Images are concrete mental representations, ways of "seeing" things, phenomena, which are resorted to recover and capture their essence, at least the details that have been relevant to the individual who constructs them. Mental models are structural analogues of the world; their structure, and not their appearance, corresponds to the structure of the situation they represent. A mental model represents a state of affairs, and consequently its structure is not arbitrary, as is that of a propositional representation (e.g., the above sentence, "the book is on the table", can refer to any book, open, closed, new, old, on any table, insofar as it is abstract and can be represented in various ways); the mental model plays a direct structural analogical representational role. Its structure reflects relevant aspects of the corresponding situation in the real or imaginary world (Moreira and Greca, 2002).

Johnson-Laird argues that instead of a mental logic -- as proposed by different psychological schools, such as, for example, Piagetian -- people use mental models to reason. These are like cognitive building blocks that can be combined or recombined as needed. The essential aspect of reasoning through models lies not only in the construction of models suitable for capturing different states of affairs but also in the ability to test whatever conclusions are reached using them. The logic, if it appears anywhere, is not in their construction, but in the testing of the conclusions, since this implies that the subject knows how to appreciate the logical importance of falsifying a conclusion and not only look for positive evidence to support it (Hampson and Morris, 1996: 243 cited by Moreira and Greca, 2002).

Reasoning that involves only one mental model can be solved quickly and correctly. However, it is very difficult to draw accurate conclusions based on premises that can be represented by many alternative models because of the great demand that this process would place on working memory (this helps to explain, for example, many of the errors that subjects make when confronted with tasks involving syllogisms). In the case of the need to construct alternative models, the subject must keep in working memory each of the various models to draw or verify a conclusion (Sternberg, 1996: 410 cited by Moreira and Greca, 2002). Under this perspective, deductive reasoning is better interpreted as a skill than as an esoteric, abstract ability. On the other hand, one way to circumvent this limitation of working memory is to represent the information implicitly, compacting it as much as possible. But it is not possible to apply the rules of formal logic to such compacted information, since logical reasoning requires that all premises be explicit. For this reason, the theory of mental models is an alternative to theories on human reasoning, accounting, for example, for cases in which people reason efficiently in situations where the information appears to a large extent implicitly (Moreira and Greca, 2002). Mental models are finite in size and cannot directly represent an infinite domain. However, a single mental model can represent an infinite number of possible states of affairs because that model can be revised recursively. Each new descriptive assertion of a situation may involve revision of the model to incorporate it. This characteristic of mental models refers mainly to models constructed from discourse, since the latter is always indeterminate and compatible with many different states of affairs; to outline this, the mind constructs an initial model and revises it recursively as necessary. Naturally there are limits to this revision: in the last analysis, the recursive revision process is governed by the truth conditions of the discourse on which the model is based (Johnson-Laird, 1983, p. 408 cited by Moreira and Greca, 2002). In other words, the mental models that the subject generates will be revised if they do not conflict with the truth value that the individual assigns to the discourse. Mental models are composed of elements and relations that represent a specific situation in an analogous-structural manner. The structures of mental models are identical to the structures of the perceived or conceived states of affairs that the models represent. Each element of a mental model, and each structural relation, must have a symbolic role.

Mills (1959) emphasizes that men usually do not define the concerns they suffer in relation to historical changes and institutional contradictions. As a rule, they do not impute the well-being they enjoy to the great ups and downs of the society in which they live. Rarely aware of the intricate connection between the type of their own life and the course of world history, ordinary men are often ignorant of what that connection means for the kind of men they are becoming and for the kind of historical activity in which they may take part. They lack the essential mental quality to perceive the interrelation of man and society, of biography and history, of self and world.

The world in which we live through time has undergone innumerable changes, some rapid and others abrupt, where man has been unable to assimilate the totality of these changes throughout the history of mankind. In this sense, the author's thesis is oriented to man's need for a mental quality that helps him to use information and develop reason to achieve lucid recapitulations of what is happening in the world and of what is perhaps happening within them.

On the other hand, Mills (1959) points out that, in times of problems or threats, the structure of values in individuals is fundamental to understand their different responses to their environment. But to understand such responses or their counterpart requires an important intellectual effort. A mental quality that seems to promise in the most dramatic way the understanding of our own intimate realities in relation to the broader social realities.

Every individual lives from one generation to the next, in a society, living a biography, and living it within a historical succession. By the fact of living he contributes, even if only to a small extent, to shaping that society and the course of its history, even as he is shaped by society and its historical impulse.

Chapter III

FIELD APPLICATION FRAMEWORK

Frame of reference

Venezuela is in the northern part of South America, between 1 - 12° N and 59 - 73° E. It has an area of 925,670 km². The relief includes both mountainous and flat areas, and about 80% of the country is below 400 meters above sea level. In the south of Venezuela is 45% of the area of all Venezuela, with generally very old surfaces, covered mostly by very poor soils that do not allow extensive agricultural development (Pla, 1990).

It has a population of 30 million inhabitants and is divided into 24 states and several archipelagos and islands.

The climate is tropical throughout the country, with uniform temperatures (22° - 28°) that only decrease with altitude. Rainfall ranges from less than 400 mm/year in some areas in the north and center-west of the country, to more than 3500 mm/year in the southwest and south. The natural vegetation covering the different zones, mainly determined by climate and soils, ranges from a light cover of xerophytic species in the arid zones, generally very affected by geological erosion, to deciduous forests and herbaceous savanna vegetation in the semi-arid areas, to dense forests and cloud forests in the sub-humid and humid zones (Pla, 1990).

Agriculture is concentrated in semi-arid to sub-humid areas, with seasonal crops grown during the rainy season, with supplemental irrigation being used in the dry season only in a small proportion of these lands with annual or perennial crops. In arid areas, part of the land is used for intensive irrigated crops, mainly vegetables and fruit trees (Pla, 1990).

Preliminary considerations

The formulation and implementation of a successful local development strategy involves two aspects: the first is due to external factors (institutional elements) and the second is due to internal factors (local elements).

With reference to the first aspect, the institutional aspect plays a very relevant role, as some key institutions will create a favourable scenario to promote any local initiative. In Venezuela there are three key institutions: National Land Institute (INTi), National Institute for Rural Development (INDER) and Agricultural Bank (BA), these institutions acting separately would be unlikely to promote community development initiatives, if on the contrary they would interact the impact would be significant, since INTi would be in charge of providing land to the peasant and the indigenous, Once access to land is assured and depending on the agro-ecological conditions and with the full consent of the social subjects, INDER can undertake a training and infrastructure improvement program and finally, with access to land, infrastructure and training, the BA can grant a line of community or individual financing. These guidelines would be the initial premises for formulating a local development strategy with emphasis on the institutional aspect. However, the strategy formulation process may have difficulties in the step in which the social subject is trained, and the infrastructure of its territorial space is improved in its different modalities, since the technician may approach the situation in a reductionist way and consequently frustrate the progress towards the next aspect such as the formulation of the strategy centered on the social subject. In this sense, a series of guidelines that the technician must follow for the correct progress towards the next aspect are detailed. It is important to mention that the theoretical position addressed in this work will allow a better understanding of the guidelines.

Analysis of the local rural space

1. Main productive activities
2. Characterize the main productive activities under a multidimensional approach
3. Support infrastructure for the main productive activities

4. Identify if the local territory has other potentialities:
   Exploitable resources

5. Main support for productive activities (if any)

6. Existence of multisectoral or differentiated public
   policies.

7. Characterize the institutional coordination of support to
   the main productive activities.

8. Characterize the household unit

   ☐ The existence of means of production

   ☐ The internal organization of labor

   ☐ Main productive activity and allocation of resources
   in the productive process

   ☐ Complementary productive activities

   ☐ Product and destination

   ☐ Organization of production in the year

   ☐ Income by productive activity

9. Characterize the production unit

10. Type of function performed by the production unit

   ☐ Economic

   ☐ Social

   ☐ Cultural

   ☐ Environmental

   ☐ Political

11. Description of the articulating axis of the production unit.

    ☐ Characterization of the local knowledge system

How to elaborate local development strategies

This section does not intend to provide a recipe book for the elaboration of development strategies, but rather a guide that will allow the technician to take advantage of the potential of the local rural area and its people and to obtain the basic elements necessary to elaborate or strengthen local strategic guidelines.

Perform a spatio-temporal analysis

1. Characterize the territory

    ☐ Climate

    ☐ Vegetation

    ☐ Fauna

    ☐ Water

    ☐ Geology

    ☐ Soil

    ☐ Land use

2. Biography of the locality

    ☐ Literature review

    ☐ Key informant interviews

    ☐ Visualize the existence of conflicts and their antecedents

☐ Visualize the existence of internal cooperation and organization and its antecedents

To have a space to live together with the social subjects.

Carry out a participatory diagnosis

Verify the facts (the facts must be observable)

Characterize the problem and locate the problem

1. Delimit the territory

2. The role of social actors in the territory

3. To know the norms and traditions of the social actors.

4. To identify power relations

5. To describe the interactions between individuals

6. Observe who has the upper hand in such interaction

7. Type of strategy to be developed: conflict or coordination.

Perform a SWOT analysis

1. Identify areas of opportunity in the short and medium term.

2. Identify critical points in the short and medium term.

3. Elaborate the strategy

4. Basic elements of the strategy developed

    ☐ The objective for which the strategy is formulated

    ☐ The resources envisaged to mobilize the strategy

    ☐ The implementation of the strategy

REFERENCES

Bautista, J. A. 2004. Sostenibilidad y agroindustria del agave en las unidades socioeconómicas campesinas de los Valles Centrales de Oaxaca. Tesis Doctoral. Colegio de Postgraduados. Puebla. 207 p.

Canzanelli, G. 2004. Valorización del potencial endógeno, competitividad territorial y lucha contra la pobreza. Center Internacional and Regional Cooperation for local economies (CIRCLE). Universidad Federico II de Nápoles. Paper N° 1. 40 p.

Díaz Tepepa, M.G; Ortiz Báez, P y I. Núñez Ramírez. 2004. Interculturalidad, saberes campesinos y educación. Colegio de Tlaxcala-Fundación Böll-SEFOA. Tlaxcala. 209 p.

Freire, P. 1998. ¿Extensión o comunicación?: la concientización en el medio rural. 21ª. Edición. Siglo XXI. México, D.F. 109 p.

INSTITUTO NACIONAL DE DESARROLLO RURAL (INDER). 2006. Acerca de la institución. Disponible *En*: http://www.inder.gov.ve.

INSTITUTO LATINOAMERICANO Y DEL CARIBE DE PLANIFICACIÓN ECONOMICA Y SOCIAL (ILPES). 1998. Manual de Desarrollo Local.

Documento: LC/IP/L.155. Dirección de Desarrollo y Gestión Local. Santiago de Chile. 201 p.

INSTITUTO NACIONAL DE TIERRAS (INTi). 2006. Banco Agrícola contribuirá a eliminar el latifundio en el país y el Decreto sobre reorganización de la tenencia y uso de las tierras con vocación agrícola. Caracas. Disponible *En*: http://www.inti.gov.ve.

Martínez Valdez, G. 1970. Plan Puebla: estrategias para aumentar la productividad en zonas de minifundios. Documento del Colegio de Postgraduados. Puebla. 121 p.

Méndez Espinoza, J. A. 2005. Transformaciones territoriales y estrategias de supervivencia en la región Soconusco del estado de Chiapas, México. Tesis de Doctorado. Universidad de Barcelona. Barcelona. 298 p.

MINISTERIO DEL INTERIOR DE CHILE (MIC). 2004. Guía metodológica Sistema de Gestión Territorial Integrada. Documento de trabajo. Santiago de Chile. 35 p.

Pla, I. 1990. La degradación y el desarrollo agrícola de Venezuela. Agronomía Tropical. 40(1-3):7-27.

Robledo Hernández, G. P. 2002. Religiosidad y estrategias de reproducción de los grupos domésticos en una comunidad indígena. Tesis de Doctorado. El Colegio de la Frontera Sur. Chiapas. 167 p.

Silva Lira, I. 2003. Metodología para la elaboración de Estrategias de Desarrollo Local. Documento: LC/IP/L.239. Nº 42. Dirección de Gestión de Desarrollo Local y Regional. Santiago de Chile. 64 p.

UNIÓN EUROPEA (EU), 2000b. La competitividad económica. Cuaderno de la innovación Nº 6. Fascículo Nº 4. Observatorio Europeo LEADER/AEIDL. 53 p.

UNIÓN EUROPEA (EU), 2001. La competitividad de los territorios rurales a escala global. Cuaderno de la innovación Nº 6. Fascículo Nº 5. Observatorio Europeo LEADER/AEIDL. 57 p.

UNIÓN EUROPEA (UE), 2000a. La competitividad social. Cuaderno de la innovación Nº 6. Fascículo Nº 2. Observatorio Europeo LEADER/AEIDL. 41 p.

Tse-Tung. M. 1967. Problemas estratégicos de la guerra revolucionaria en china. *En*: Selección de Escritos Militares. Ed. en lenguas extranjeras.

Mintzberg. H. 1991. Elaboración artesanal de la estrategia. *En*: Mintzberg y La Dirección. Ed. Díaz Santos. Madrid.

Bourdieu, P. 2002. Razones prácticas: sobre la teoría de la acción. Ed. Anagrama. Barcelona. 232 p.

Teubal, Miguel. 2001. Globalización y nueva ruralidad en América Latina. *En:* ¿Una nueva ruralidad en América Latina?. Texto compilado por Norma Giarracca. Consejo

Latinoamericano de Ciencias Sociales (CLACSO) y Agencia Sueca de Desarrollo Internacional (ASDI). Buenos Aires. 363 pp. Disponible *En:* www.clacso.edu.ar y www.clacso.org.

Pérez, Edelmira. 2001. Hacia una nueva visión de lo rural. *En:* ¿Una nueva ruralidad en América Latina? Texto compilado por Norma Giarracca. Consejo Latinoamericano de Ciencias Sociales (CLACSO) y Agencia Sueca de Desarrollo Internacional (ASDI). Buenos Aires. 363 pp. Disponible *En:* www.clacso.edu.ar y www.clacso.org.

Linck, T. 2001. El campo en la ciudad: reflexiones en torno a las ruralidades emergentes. Estudios Agrarios. Revista de la Procuraduría Agraria. 17:9-29.

FAO. 1999. El Carácter Multifuncional de la Agricultura y la Tierra. Documento Expositivo. Maastricht. Versión electrónica. 61 p.

Castells, M. 1999. La era de la información. Vol I. Ed. Siglo Veintiuno. México, D.F. 590 p.

Janvry, A y E. Sadoulet. 2004. Hacia un enfoque territorial del desarrollo rural. Documento preparado para el 4to. Foro Temático Regional de América Latina y el Caribe. Costa Rica. 21 p.

Sepúlveda, S; A, Rodríguez; R, Echeverri y M, Portilla. 2003. El Enfoque territorial del desarrollo rural. Instituto Interamericano de Cooperación para la Agricultura (IICA). San José, Costa Rica. 180 p.

Canzanelli, G. 2004. Valorización del potencial endógeno, competitividad territorial y lucha contra la pobreza. Center Internacional and Regional Cooperation for local economies (CIRCLE). Universidad Federico II de Nápoles. Paper N° 1. 40 p.

Archetti, E. P. 1978. Una visión de los estudios sobre el campesinado. Cuadernos Agrarios. Chapingo. Mexico, D.F. 6:25-51.

Deere, C y A. Janvry. 1992 Marco conceptual para el análisis emperico de los campesinos. Disponible *En:* www.clades.cl/2/rev2art1.htm.

Bartra, A. 1998. Globalización, crisis, y desarrollo rural en América Latina. Asociación Latinoamericana de Sociología Rural (ALASRU). V Congreso Latinoamericano de Sociología Rural. Memorias. Mexico, D.F. 233 p.

Hernández, R. s/f. Teorías sobre campesinado en América Latina: Una evaluación crítica. Rev. Chilena de Antropología. No. 12. Disponible *En:*

http://www.antropoenfermeria.com/textos%20antropo
logia/teorias%20sobre%20campesinado.htm.

Thorner, D. 1979. La economía campesina. Concepto para la historia económica. *En:* Economía Campesina, Centro de Estudios y Promoción del Desarrollo (DESCO). Lima. 139-153 p.

Portilla Rodríguez, M. 2003. Actores sociales en el desarrollo rural territorial. Instituto Interamericano de Cooperación para la Agricultura (IICA). Sinopsis N° 8.

Bello, A. 2004. Etnicidad y ciudadanía en América Latina: la acción colectiva de los pueblos indígenas. Comisión Económica para América Latina y el Caribe (CEPAL) y la Sociedad Alemana de Cooperación Técnica (GTZ). Santiago de Chile. 222 p.

Carlsen, L. 1999. Autonomía indígena y usos y costumbres: la innovación de la tradición. Rev. Chiapas. 7:1-19. Disponible *En*: http://www.ezln.org/revistachiapas/ No7/ch7carlsen.html.

______, **1978**. El indigenismo y la cultura: un marco general de análisis. Rev. Enfoques colombianos. 11:1-16. Disponible *En*: http://www.colciencias.gov.co/ seiaal/documentos/lgvu16.htm.

Ávila Méndez, A. 2002. Organización social, autoridades indígenas y reforma constitucional. Instituto Nacional Indigenista. Boletín. Nueva Época. 1 (3): 1-11.

Mills, C. W. 1959. La imaginación sociológica. 1ª Ed. Fondo de Cultura Económica. México, D.F. 23-43 pp.

Moreira, M. A y I. M. Greca. 2002. Mental models and conceptual models in the teaching & learning of science. Rev. Bras. de Investigacion em Educação em Ciências. 2 (3):84-96.

MINISTERIO DE EDUCACION, CULTURA Y DEPORTES (MECD). 2003. Avances y perspectivas de la Dirección de Asuntos Indígenas. Documento de Trabajo. Caracas. 13 pp.

Molina, L. E. 1996. Cambio en los patrones espaciales de la agricultura venezolana (1970-1990). Agroalimentaria. 3: 1-10.

Ríos, J y Carvallo, G. 1990. Análisis histórico de la organización del espacio en Venezuela. Ed. Consejo de Desarrollo Científico y Humanístico (UCV). Caracas. 58 p.

González, B; Peña, M; Rincón, N; Bustillo, L y F. Urdaneta. 2004. Formulación de lineamientos estratégicos para el desarrollo rural, basado en una

metodología participativa. Rev. Fac. Agron. (LUZ). 21:
395-410.

Delgado Barrios, J. C. 2003. Estrategias metodológicas
para la construcción de redes comunitarias agrícolas en
pro del desarrollo local. Caso: productores de plátanos del
sur del lago de Maracaibo. Venezuela. Agroalimentaria.
17: 29-38.